THE GREAT BOOK OF

CASTLES

CASTLES

Text by John Monks

Rourke Enterprises, Inc.
Vero Beach, FL 32964

117 5116

Library of Congress Cataloging-in-Publication Data

Monks, John, 1957–
  The great book of castles/John Monks.

    p.   cm.
    Includes index.
    Summary: Describes the structures and functions of castles and
everyday life inside a medieval castle.
    ISBN 0-86592-456-2
    1. Castles—Europe—Juvenile literature.
2. Castles—Middle East—Juvenile literature.
[1. Castles.   2. Civilization, Medieval.]
I. Title.
UG428.M65   1988
355.7'094—dc19   87-35646
                                                         CIP
                                                          AC

Contents

The First Castles

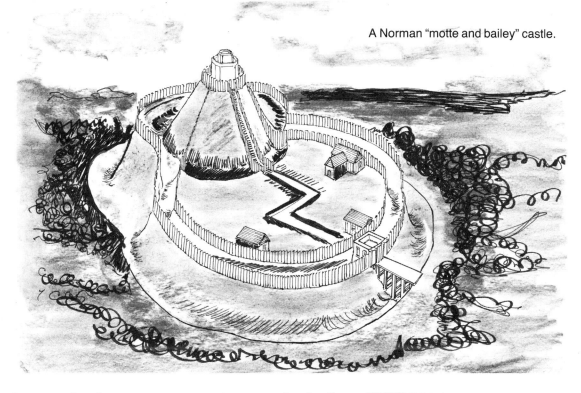

A Norman "motte and bailey" castle.

Thousands of years ago primitive peoples built wooden stockades to protect themselves from wild animals and warring tribes. When possible, they built them on hills or cliff tops so they could spot approaching enemies. It was also easier to defend a stockade built on high ground. The attackers had to slither up steep and muddy banks while being bombarded with rocks, spears and arrows.

Strong timber walls were built to protect their huts and the entrance was defended by stout wooden gates. Quite often, deep ditches were dug around the stockade to make it more difficult to reach the walls of the village.

In peaceful times, people farmed the surrounding countryside and hunted in nearby forests. But when their community was under attack, they would bring their families and animals into the stockade for safety. There would always be water and food stores to keep them alive until the battle was over.

The Ancient Greeks understood the importance of fortifying their towns and cities. The fortress at Mycenae, which dates as far back as 1500 BC. shows how they built with defense in mind.

6

The Bayeux Tapestry.

Unlike these early fortified villages that were built for defensive reasons, the Romans built huge fortresses to station their advancing armies. These were usually rectangular in shape and, like the stockades, were surrounded by deep ditches and had high watchtowers along the walls. At first they were temporary wooden fortresses to protect their camps, but as the Romans became established they used stone to fortify their towns and military camps. As the Roman Empire grew larger, its frontiers became much more difficult to defend. The Romans tried to solve this by building individual forts connected by long thick walls. A good example is Hadrian's Wall in the north of England, which was erected to keep out the Picts and the Scots.

When the Normans (from northern France) invaded England in 1066 they quickly began building simple earth and timber castles to protect themselves from the defeated Anglo-Saxons. So desperate was William the Conqueror, the Norman king, to keep control of his new kingdom that he ordered all of his barons to build castles at strategic points all over the country. These castles were built quickly because the Normans expected to be attacked at any time. The defeated Anglo-Saxons were used as slave labor. First they had to build a huge mound of earth, called a "motte," on top of which was built a wooden tower, the "keep." The motte was connected to a courtyard, called the "bailey," by a sloping bridge. The bailey, which housed the stables and storehouses, was enclosed by a high wooden fence. Again, the whole construction was surrounded by a deep ditch to make it more secure.

Most early Norman castles were made of wood. But in areas where trees were scarce the keep was made entirely of stone, like the one at Totnes in southwest England

How Castles got Bigger and Better

The Normans realized that their simple earth and timber forts would not be strong enough to withstand any prolonged attacks by the defeated Anglo-Saxons. Timber can be easily destroyed by fire, and it also rots very quickly. The Normans replaced the wooden fences and buildings of their "motte and bailey" castles with stone towers and walls.

One of the first – and most famous – Norman stone "keeps" is the White Tower, which is still the centerpiece of the Tower of London. It is named so because the walls were regularly whitewashed. The tower was originally intended as a royal residence for William the Conqueror, but he died before it was completed. It also served as an awesome reminder to the citizens of London as to who their new rulers were.

The White Tower, unlike in Norman times, now stands in the center of the Tower of London as successive royal builders added to its defenses.

Caerphilly Castle, Wales.

Norman castles can be easily recognized by their rectangular keep, like the one at Rochester in England.

Throughout the twelfth and thirteenth centuries the shape and size of European castles gradually changed. The rectangular keeps introduced by the Normans were replaced by round ones, which proved to be much stronger under attack.

As armies discovered more efficient ways of breaching a castle, designers started to build castles with thick outer walls and rounded towers at each corner.

The Norman idea of the keep as a place to house the baron or lord of the castle, or as a place to hide if the enemy broke through also died out. The castle owner, his family, and barons now lived in a main hall in the bailey, or central courtyard.

Soldiers who had been fighting religious wars in the Holy Land returned to Europe with stories about the huge fortresses and walled cities they had seen. As a result, castles were built with yet another line of defense – an immense outer wall that circled the whole castle. There are many examples of these "concentric" castles in Europe.

All Shapes and Sizes

Harlech Castle in Wales is a good example of a concentric castle.
Edward I had it built toward the end of the thirteenth century to keep
order in his newly conquered territory. In all, about one thousand
laborers and craftsmen were employed to build it.

Small castles

The people who lived on the border of Scotland and England often built simple fortified houses, called Pele towers, for protection in times of war.

Angers Castle, on the Loire in France, has D-shaped towers.

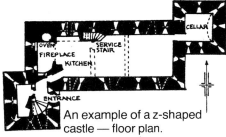

An example of a z-shaped castle — floor plan.

Big castles

Sometimes whole cities were fortified with huge walls and towers, like Carcassone in southeastern France.

The Medieval Castle

During the Middle Ages (the period of history roughly spanning 1000–1500 A.D.), castles of all shapes and sizes were built. Usually monarchs, princes, and noblemen built castles to protect their goods and land from invading armies, and sometimes from their own people. In this period, the castle developed from a simple wooden or stone tower into a complicated fortress that required the building skills of thousands of laborers and craftsmen.

Unlike the buildings in our modern cities, which are torn down when they fall into disuse, medieval castles underwent gradual changes and modification. Many of the castles that are still standing in Europe started off as Roman forts, originally built because they were situated in strong defensive positions.

Bodiam Castle, England.

The largest and probably the liveliest room in a medieval castle was the great hall. This is where the king or baron and his knights ate their meals and where great banquets were held when important noblemen came to stay. The walls of the great hall were painted in bright colors or draped with tapestries.

Next to the hall was the great chamber (also called the "solar") which was the baron's private apartment. Here he and his family slept and kept their private belongings. Another smaller room, the "wardrobe," was used as a changing room and a place to store clothes.

Religion was an important part of everyday life in the Middle Ages. Every castle had a chapel where morning and evening mass was held.

Large kitchens, sometimes built as separate buildings in the bailey because of the fire risk, were another important part of a castle. Here cooks prepared food for the baron and the soldiers of the garrison.

Food and provisions were kept in a storeroom, which was usually in the coolest part of the castle on the ground floor or in the basement. Ale and wine was stored in a room called the "buttery." This name has nothing to do with butter but comes instead from the French word *bouteille*, meaning bottle.

The armory was where the weapons were stored. Bows and arrows, crossbows, and swords had to be kept in good order in case the castle was attacked.

Toilets, or "privies" as they were called, were small cubicles built into the towers above drainage shafts that emptied into a ditch below.

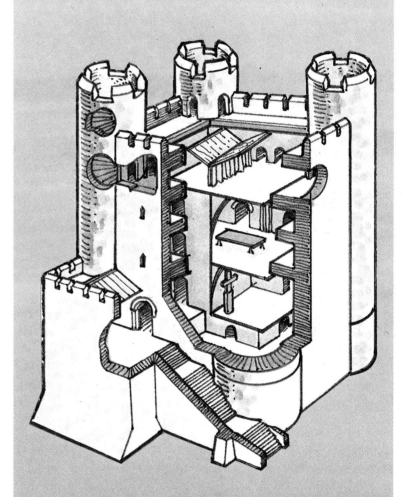

The Castle's Defenses

One of the best ways of making a castle more difficult to attack was to surround it with a ditch filled with water. This was called a "moat".

The main gate, usually the only way in and out of a castle, was called the "drawbridge". When under attack, the drawbridge could be closed very quickly, leaving the castle entirely surrounded by water.

The entrance was the weakest part of a castle, and it was often strengthened by building a stone tower, called a "gatehouse". This contained an inner gate (a "portcullis") which could be lowered by means of a rope wound around a winch in the room above. In peacetime, the portcullis would be left up, but it would come crashing down if the entrance was attacked.

If enemy soldiers did manage to get over the drawbridge into the gatehouse, boiling water and rocks would be dropped onto them through "murder holes" in the roof above the entrance passageway.

Later castles had a building on the other side of the moat, too. This building, called a "barbican," protected the approach to the castle's main entrance.

The barbican at Lewes castle in Sussex, England

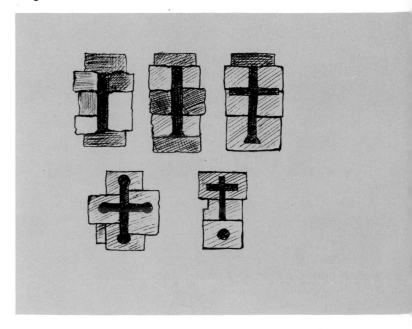

Leeds Castle, Kent, England.

Most castle walls had slits in them called "arrow loops" through which archers could fire at their attackers. The openings were very narrow on the outer wall but wide on the inside. The soldier could get a good view of his target and at the same time was protected. A boy reloaded a second bow while the archer was firing.

The top section of a castle's walls, the "battlements," had gaps in them through which soldiers could fire arrows and throw rocks. A long wooden platform, called a "wallwalk," was built behind the battlements to support the soldiers and sentries.

To make it easier for the soldiers defending a castle to fire at men attacking the walls below, wooden "hoardings" were erected. These jutted out from the battlements and gave the defenders a much clearer view of what was happening down below. Since the wooden hoardings could be easily set on fire, they were often replaced by permanent stone parapets called "machicolations".

As well as firing arrows at their enemies, and dropping rocks and boiling water onto them, soldiers defending a castle also poured a sticky substance called "Greek fire" onto their attackers. No one knows exactly how it was made but, according to medieval chronicles, it could burn soldiers alive inside their armor!

The Castle Under Attack

Castles played a key role in medieval warfare because they defended important territory such as mountain passes, river crossings, and towns. If an advancing army wanted to conquer these areas, it first had to capture the castle.

The attackers' first move was usually to try to smash through the walls and gates and attempt to scale the battlements. They would also surround the castle to stop any deliveries of food, water, and weapons. When the supplies inside the castle eventually ran out, the castle defenders would have to surrender. This sort of attack, or siege, could last for months and, in some cases, years.

If these methods did not work, the attackers sometimes resorted to blackmail and bribery. They might threaten to hang an important hostage if the garrison did not surrender. Or else they might try to bribe someone inside the castle to betray his companions and open the gates.

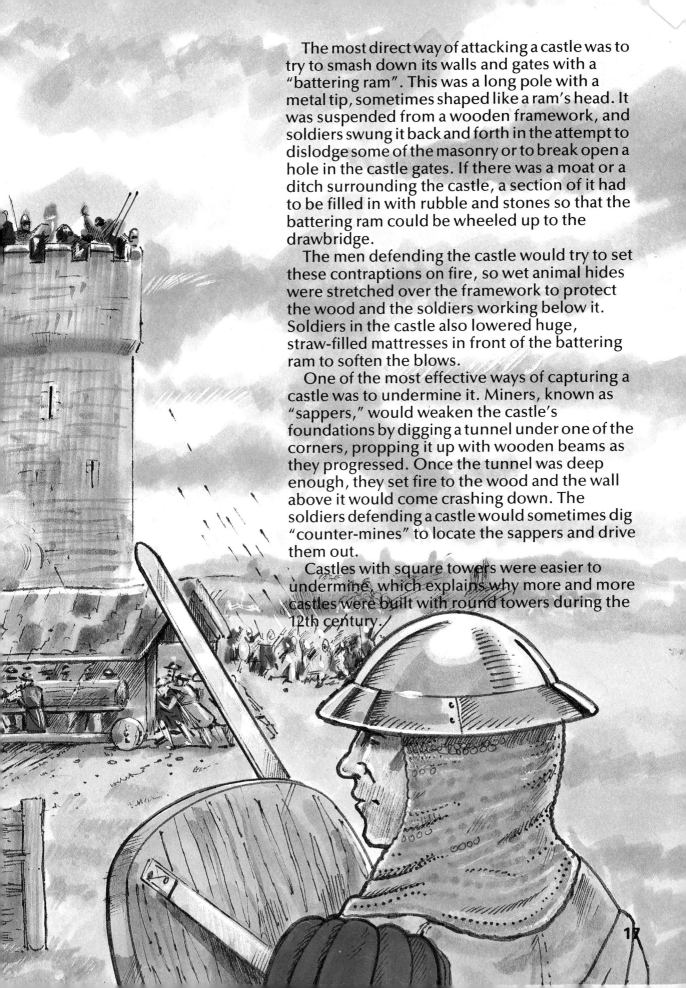

The most direct way of attacking a castle was to try to smash down its walls and gates with a "battering ram". This was a long pole with a metal tip, sometimes shaped like a ram's head. It was suspended from a wooden framework, and soldiers swung it back and forth in the attempt to dislodge some of the masonry or to break open a hole in the castle gates. If there was a moat or a ditch surrounding the castle, a section of it had to be filled in with rubble and stones so that the battering ram could be wheeled up to the drawbridge.

The men defending the castle would try to set these contraptions on fire, so wet animal hides were stretched over the framework to protect the wood and the soldiers working below it. Soldiers in the castle also lowered huge, straw-filled mattresses in front of the battering ram to soften the blows.

One of the most effective ways of capturing a castle was to undermine it. Miners, known as "sappers," would weaken the castle's foundations by digging a tunnel under one of the corners, propping it up with wooden beams as they progressed. Once the tunnel was deep enough, they set fire to the wood and the wall above it would come crashing down. The soldiers defending a castle would sometimes dig "counter-mines" to locate the sappers and drive them out.

Castles with square towers were easier to undermine, which explains why more and more castles were built with round towers during the 12th century.

17

Long ladders were propped up against the castle walls so that soldiers could try to climb over the battlements. This must have been the riskiest form of attack, since the men up above could fire arrows and hurl rocks at the soldiers climbing the ladders.

Another method of attack was to construct a gigantic wooden tower, called a "siege tower" or "belfry", which could be wheeled up to the castle's walls. Archers could then fire at the soldiers defending the battlements. Siege towers, too, were protected with wet animal skins.

War Machines

Two types of rock-throwing machines were used to bombard castles. The "mangonel" was a huge wooden catapult that could hurl rocks and fireballs through the air at terrific speed.

A later machine, the "trébuchet", was a giant sling. Its huge arm, holding a large rock in a net, was winched down. When released, a counterweight would cause the beam to fly up and hurl the rock through the air.

Sometimes the severed heads of prisoners and dead horses were fired over a castle's walls to spread terror and disease.

The long wooden beam, which held the rock, was held down with strong animal sinews. When released, the wooden arm would fly up, shooting the rock over the castle walls.

Knights, Soldiers and Their Weapons

King Arthur's Table, Winchester, England.

Medieval knights were the king's elite group of warriors. In Norman times they wore a type of armor called "chain mail", made of small metal rings joined together to form a tunic called a "hauberk." They also wore metal helmets with strips of metal at the front to protect their noses. Chain mail gave some protection in battle but was not strong enough to withstand piercing blows from an enemy's sword or arrows fired from a crossbow.

In the 13th and 14th centuries, knights wore complete suits of armor made of metal plates shaped to different parts of their body. Their helmets, or "visors," were fitted with slits to see through.

In the confusion of battle it was important to be able to tell friend from foe, so knights painted their coat-of-arms on their shields, flags, and banners. Knights who fought in the Holy Land were called Crusaders and wore the cross of Jesus on their tunics.

One of the most lethal weapons used by soldiers defending a castle was the crossbow. The archer had to be very strong to pull back the thick cord that fired the bolt. Crossbows were very accurate and very powerful Their arrows could pierce a man's shield and armor and come out the other side.

One type of crossbow that became popular had a metal ratchet to tighten the cord. Even the weakest person in the garrison could load this.

Archers also fought with short bows, which could be fired much more quickly than a crossbow. By the 14th century, the Welsh longbow was being used. As the name suggests, this bow was larger and more powerful. A good archer could have five arrows in the air at one time!

The common foot-soldier did not wear armor or ride a horse. Instead he had a leather tunic for protection and fought with a sword or pike.

Knights always went into battle on horseback and fought with swords, lances, and iron maces.

Fun and Games

Life wasn't all work and no play in a castle. On special occasions – perhaps when the baron and his lady had to entertain guests – a huge banquet would be held. Today much of the food that was eaten at these events, such as peacocks, swans, and wild boar, would appear strange.

A king or lord of a castle might have his own jester, who told jokes and amused the guests. Singing minstrels and musicians would play from a gallery above the great hall. At the same time acrobats and jugglers would be performing on the main floor.

Hunting was the nobility's favorite pastime. The king and his men rode into the forests in search of hares, rabbits, wild boar and deer. Anybody caught poaching was punished very severely. Falconry was another favorite aristocratic sport.

On a parade ground in front of the castle, the baron and his knights would hold jousting tournaments. Mounted knights in their glittering suits of armor would charge at each other with blunted lances. These mock battles provided entertainment and military training.

The aim was not to kill your opponent but to knock him off his horse. Many such tournaments were held all over Europe, and knights came from far and wide to take part in them. If two knights did have a serious quarrel with each other, then they would have a fight to the death.

The Castle Hierarchy

Members of the nobility, especially the king or queen, did not live in the same residence year-round. They would travel from castle to castle to inspect their lands and to keep an eye on their barons.

A **castellan** or **constable** was the man who was left in charge of the castle when the king or baron was away. His job was to ensure that the castle was well stocked and in good order.

The **steward** acted as the baron's deputy in his absence. He had to appoint officials, hold court, and look after the accounts.

The **marshal** organized the traveling arrangements of the household when moving from one castle to another. He also had to make sure that the garrison was well trained and well disciplined.

Squires were the sons of noble parents who were sent to castles to be trained in knightly manners and behavior. This was called "chivalry."

Daily Life in a Castle

A castle wasn't just for fighting wars. It was also a home. Everyone who lived and worked in castles had different tasks and jobs, so they must have been very lively places.

Every day, bread was baked, firewood collected, and meals prepared. Carpenters and stonemasons were busy repairing parts of the castle, tailors making new clothes, and soldiers practicing their fighting skills in the courtyard. Even small castles had craftspeople: saddlers, shoemakers, and weavers. Coopers made barrels for wine and beer, fletchers made arrows, and smiths shoed the horses.

Farmyard animals such as pigs and chickens roamed free in the bailey. The garrison's horses were groomed and exercised in the courtyards and kept in the stables.

There were few carpets in those days, so the stone floors were covered with reeds and wild herbs. The garbage was thrown into the moat or a ditch called the "midden" and left to rot. Fireplaces were only introduced in later castles, so the air in early castles must have been thick with smoke from open fires. There was no glass in the windows, because it was very rare and expensive to make. All in all, castles must have been hot and smelly during the summer months and bitterly cold in the winter.

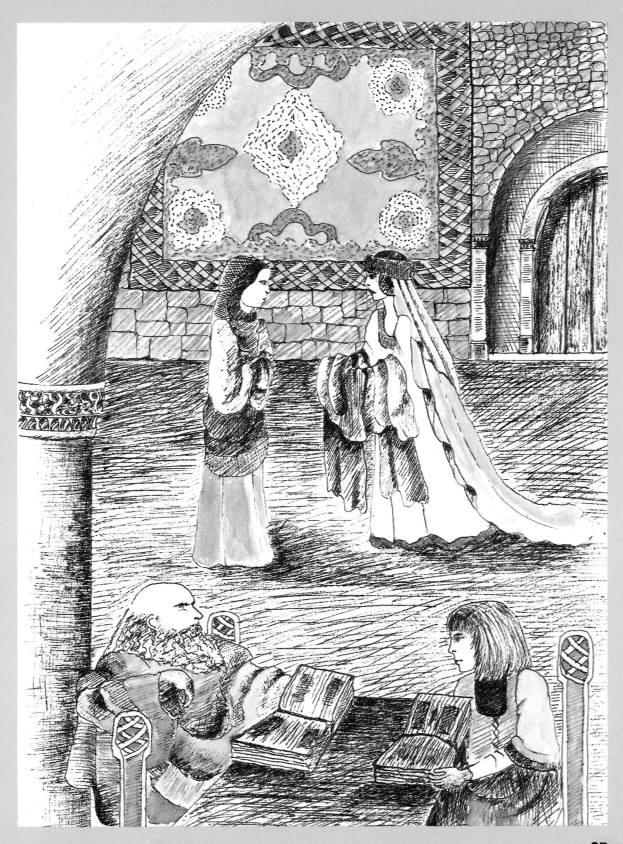

How Castles Were Built

Early timber forts could be erected in a matter of weeks but the much larger stone castles often took years to build.

The first step was to choose a suitable site, preferably on high ground or near a stream or river that could be diverted to supply the moat. Also, castles were often situated near fertile land so that food was readily available.

Once the site had been cleared of trees and leveled out, the ditch or moat was dug. Then, the foundations were dug so that the walls and towers would have a firm base. When the main defenses had been finished, the wallwalks and wooden buildings in the courtyard were built.

Thousands of workmen were needed: masons, stone-cutters, quarriers, smiths, and plasterers, as well as general laborers. They used carts, wagons, and boats to transport materials to the building site.

At the end of the 13th century, Edward I of England built a chain of castles around Wales to keep firm control over his newly conquered territory. Workmen were brought from all over the country. Although many of them were forced into service, they received a daily wage.

Beaumaris was the last, and the grandest, of Edward I's great Welsh castles. Unfortunately, it was never completed, because there wasn't enough money left to pay for labor or materials.

Some of the tools the men used can still be seen today – hammers, pickaxes, spades, and saws. They carried earth and cement in large baskets, which they hauled to the top of the walls with hoists and pulleys.

The type of rock used varied from castle to castle, depending on what was locally available. The earliest castles were made of small square stones, and later ones were made of large rectangular blocks.

Many later castles were made of brick, like the one at Herstmonceux in the south of England.

Famous Sieges

In 1204 King Philip II of France besieged Chateau Gaillard, which was being held by King John's English forces.

After six months of trying to starve the garrison, the French king grew impatient and started the assault. Sappers set to work and soon brought one of the outer walls crashing down. The defenders retreated into the middle bailey.

The castle was well stocked with food and weapons, so the siege might have gone on for much longer had not some French soldiers spotted an unbarred window high up on one of the walls. They reached this by climbing up the inside of a toilet shaft.

Once inside the castle, the soldiers started shouting and hammering on the doors to give the impression that a lot of men had broken in. In the confusion that followed some of them managed to lower the drawbridge and let the French army in.

The defenders were now trapped in the inner bailey but still refused to surrender. King Philip's forces used a gigantic siege tower during the last assault and miners cracked open another wall. The defending army, which by now had been reduced to 36 knights and 120 men, was captured. One of the longest sieges in medieval history was brought to an end.

Kenilworth Castle in England held out for six months in 1266 before starvation forced the defenders to submit.

In 1215 Rochester castle held out against King John for six months before being starved into submission. In the course of the siege, sappers brought down one of the square towers by digging a tunnel, filling it with straw and the fat of forty pigs, and then igniting it.

Royal Castles

The grandest and most impressive castles are usually those that were built for monarchs. In addition to royal residences for kings and queens, castles were also symbols of their military and political power. Royal castles needed to be large enough to house the king's private staff of clerks and advisers, who helped him carry out his official duties.

No one was supposed to build a castle without the monarch's permission. But sometimes, under a weak ruler, barons defied their king's authority and tried to increase their own wealth and power. Henry II of England deliberately destroyed these unlawful castles when he was made king to stop his barons from becoming too powerful. After that, anyone wanting to build a castle or fortify their home had to apply for a licence to build.

Towards the end of the 14th century, the cannon was used more and more often in warfare. Not even the sturdiest castle could withstand a prolonged bombardment from the new artillery, so castles began to lose their importance. Battles were increasingly fought by large armies on the move rather than by long drawn-out sieges. Kings and queens now spent their money on making their castles more comfortable and decorative, changing them from imposing fortresses into stately homes and elegant palaces.

Scotney castle in England is a good example of a house that was fortified after the owner had obtained a license from the king.

The massive Castel Nuovo in Italy was built in the 13th century for Charles of Anjou, King of Sicily.

Windsor Castle in England is the largest inhabited castle in the world. Queen Elizabeth II lives there several months a year.

Saumur on the River Loire in France is a fine example of a castle that was modified to make a comfortable country residence.

The Alhambra, which dominates the city of Granada in Spain, started off as a humble hillfort and developed into the chief residence of the kings of Granada. Its courtyards contain elegant fountains, luxuriant gardens, and orchards, which contrast with the arid red rock on which it is built.

Castles as Prisons

The execution block and axe on display in the White Tower.

Kings, queens, and important members of the nobility were sometimes imprisoned in a castle's dungeons. The dungeons were usually situated in the basement and must have been damp, dark, and forbidding places. The law of the land in medieval times was often brutal. A suspected criminal was often given a choice: he could be tried by jury and be hanged if found guilty, or he could refuse a trial and be starved to death in prison. Blinding and mutilation were common punishments for crime, and torture was an accepted way of extracting information.

But it would be wrong to think that anyone who was kept prisoner in a castle was automatically tortured and killed. Very often, prisoners – especially those of noble birth – were confined in relative comfort with bedding, food, and wine, while friends or allies raised the ransom demanded for their release. Kings and barons often made large sums of money by holding a prisoner captive rather than putting him to death.

The most famous entrance of the Tower of London is Traitor's Gate, through which many royal prisoners passed after having been tried and found guilty of treason. Some of the famous and tragic figures who were executed here include Lady Jane Grey and Ann Boleyn (one of the wives of Henry VIII), Sir Walter Raleigh, and Sir Thomas Moore. The Tower of London is no longer used as a prison but is still garrisoned and has a huge collection of arms and weapons.

Many famous noblemen and women passed through Traitor's Gate on their way to execution.

In 1327 Edward II, King of England, was thrown into the dungeons at Berkeley Castle by some political opponents. His captors first threw rotting animal carcases into a room above his cell, hoping that the stench would kill him. Edward survived this for six months only to be brutally murdered.

Chateau de Chillon in Switzerland has a vaulted cellar beneath the Great Hall. A cleric called Francois Bonivard was chained to one of the pillars for six years from 1530 to 1536.

Castles Around the World

Castles can be found in most countries of the world. Some are now little more than mounds of rubble – ruins on remote windswept sites – which serve to remind us of a bygone age. Others have survived the test of time (and war) and stand as a magnificent tribute to the people who built them.

Of all the countries in the world, Spain has some of the most spectacular castles. One of them is Castel Coca in Castile. Its brickwork is elaborately decorated in a herringbone pattern but its round gun ports and arrow loops remind us of its basic purpose: war.

Castel del Monte, in southern Italy, is the most famous of the castles built by Frederick II, Holy Roman Emperor and King of Sicily. Although it looks very awesome it was built primarily as a hunting-lodge!

There is a tragic story concerning the castle's architect: so eager was Frederick II to hear news of how his castle building was progressing, that he sent a young courtier to investigate. The messenger was delayed on his way to the castle so he decided to make up a story. Arriving back at Frederick's court, he told the king that the construction work was of very poor quality. Frederick then sent an angry letter to the architect, summoning him to the capital to explain himself. Thinking himself in disgrace, the architect committed suicide in one of the rooms of the castle, which by now was nearly finished. When Frederick found out the truth he dragged the courtier to the top of the highest tower and threw him off as "a sacrifice to the memory of the architect."

In the Middle Ages, the Crusader knights who went to recapture the Holy Land from the invading Saracens built huge fortresses to protect pilgrims journeying to Jerusalem. The mighty fortress at Krak in the Middle East is the most famous of the Crusader castles. Its defenses were so complex and difficult to penetrate that the only time it was ever captured was through trickery. A letter, supposedly written by the knights' grand master, was smuggled into the castle. It said that a relief army would not be sent and told them to surrender. This the knights did – only to find that the letter was a forgery.

Unlike their European counterparts, German castles were often no more than towers used as places of refuge from bandits and warring soldiers.

The great German emperor, Frederick I Barbarossa built many fine castles but the emphasis was on elegance and decoration rather than thick defensive walls. Quite often, German castles were built on such inaccessible sites that defensive measures were not necessary anyway.

Kokorin Castle, Czechoslovakia.

Citadel of Van, a natural fortress, Turkey.

The Pfalz, on the River Rhine, served as a toll collecting station for passing boats.

When the Moguls from Persia conquered Delhi in the 17th century, they built the Red Fort.

Valencia Castle, Spain.

Haunted Castles

The ghostly figure of Anne Boleyn, executed on the orders of her husband Henry VIII, has been seen gliding over the bridge in the grounds of Hever Castle in England. She usually appears on Christmas Eve.

Most castles have ghosts, especially those associated with dark deeds and gruesome murders. Hauntings take different forms: screeches in the night, ghostly echoes, strange apparitions, or just a creepy atmosphere!

One of Windsor Castle's most famous ghosts is Henry VIII. In his old age, Henry became very fat, and terrible sores on his legs caused him to limp. His wheezing breath and weary shuffling walk can still be heard in many of the castle's corridors.

One of the world's most haunted castles is Glamis in Scotland. Visitors have often reported hearing strange knocking sounds coming from the walls. One explanation goes back hundreds of years to when some men of the Ogilvie clan were locked inside a remote room after seeking refuge during a clan war.

Lord Strathmore, who lived there in the last century discovered this hidden room. When he forced open the ancient door, he fainted at what he saw: a mound of skeletons, some of which still had the bones of their arms between their teeth as they tried to ward off death by eating their own flesh.

In 1264 Blanche de Warrene was betrothed to Sir Ralph de Capo, lord of Rochester Castle. In the same year, the castle was besieged by Sir Gilbert de Clare, who had been rejected by Lady Blanche. The soldiers defending the castle fought well and Sir Gilbert finally gave up the siege. But as his army retreated, Sir Ralph and his knights lowered the drawbridge and charged out of the castle to chase the defeated soldiers.

In the confusion of battle, Sir Gilbert realized that Lady Blanche was alone in the castle and saw a chance of revenge. He slipped back to the castle walls and climbed over the battlements where Lady Blanche was watching the distant fighting. Realizing she was in great danger, Lady Blanche barricaded herself in the top of the round tower but Sir Gilbert soon smashed the door down with his battleaxe.

By this time, Sir Ralph had spotted the two struggling figures on the top of the tower. From the battlefield he fired an arrow at Sir Gilbert. Tragically, it was deflected off his armor straight into the heart of Lady Blanche. She died, realizing that her lover had accidentally killed her.

Her sad figure is still seen today walking the battlements, weeping at her cruel destiny.

41

Cinderella's Castle: A Fairy Tale Come True

Imagine a castle with air-conditioned rooms instead of cold drafty chambers, elevators instead of steep spiral staircases, and modern kitchens in place of smoky banquet halls. This is Cinderella's Castle in Walt Disney World's Magic Kingdom in Florida. It's a fairy tale castle in every way, with golden spires 200 feet high, a glittering moat, and a sweeping promenade curving over the water to an arched portcullis.

The castle design goes back to France, where the famous story originated. After studying the famous palaces at Fontainébleau and Versailles, the designers created an ancient castle with all the comforts of space-age America. Instead of dark, dank dungeons, there are service tunnels providing underground connections to other parts of the Magic Kingdom. Visitors can travel to the parapet level restaurant by a winding stairway or an automatic elevator complete with built-in creaks!

Ten slender towers up to 90 feet high were pre-fabricated near the site, then slated, gilded, and hoisted into place. Five glittering glass mosaic murals in the foyer of the 18 story castle vividly depict the classic Cinderella fairy tale. The fairy godmother still changes into a pumpkin in the royal coach, the glass slipper still fits the little cinder girl who goes on to win the handsome prince. The murals are made of fine jewel like pieces of Italian glass, some of them fused together with silver and 14 carat gold.

Walt Disney World's Cinderella Castle in Florida gives everyone the chance to step into a fairy tale.

The inspiration for Disneyland's first castle, built 16 years ago in California, came from English and German palaces.

43

Modern Castles

In the nineteenth century, many people started to take a renewed interest in castles. Rich people, who had made money in the new industries in the cities, wanted their own stately homes in the country. Some of them renovated castles that had lain in ruins for centuries, while others built their own from scratch.

One of the most famous builders of imitation castles was Ludwig II, King of Bavaria in southern Germany. He was fascinated by medieval German legends and built a series of castles in an attempt to recreate what he thought was the Golden Age. His most famous castle is Neuschwanstein, built in an idyllic setting on a steep rock overlooking a lake, with the Alps in the background. Ludwig spent only one hundred days in his "fairy tale" castle. The Bavarian government, nearly bankrupted by the huge spending on his castles, declared him mad. Shortly after being deposed he supposedly committed suicide by drowning in the lake at the foot of the castle.

Wealthy people have continued to build castles in this century. Castle Drogo in England was completed in 1930. It was intended to be a stately home.

Castle Coch in Wales was reconstructed, at great expense, in the 19th century.

Glossary

Barbican   A fortified construction built to protect the entrance to a castle.

Battlements   The top section of a castle's walls with openings to fire arrows or guns.

Buttery   The room where wine, beer and other drinks were kept.

Concentric castle   A fortress ringed by a series of outer walls for extra defense.

Crenellated   Describes castle walls built with gaps (crenels) at regular intervals along the top. The solid parts, behind which the defenders are called "merlons".

Drawbridge   Usually the main gate to a castle, which can be drawn up or let down, leaving a gap over the ditch to stop the enemy from advancing.

Herringbone   Brickwork in which stones or tiles are laid in alternate rows, producing a pattern like the bones of a herring.

Hoarding   Wooden gallery overhanging the top of a castle's walls to enable defenders to drop things on people below.

Keep   The main stronghold (usually a tower) of a castle (sometimes called a "donjon").

Portcullis   Iron gate which could be lowered when the castle was under attack. Usually situated in the gatehouse.

Solar   Private room for the lord and his family.

Bailey   The area inside a castle that is enclosed by a wall. It usually contained the out-buildings such as kitchens and stables.

Squire   A boy who served a knight in preparation for becoming a knight himself.

Moat   Channel encircling a castle that was filled with water.

Mangonel   A mechanical sling that could hurl rocks and stones.

Joust   A mock battle between knights using horses and lances.

Index

Acknowledgements

We would like to thank and acknowledge the following people for the use of their photographs and transparancies.

p. 6/7	British Tourist Authority Ronald Sheridan
p. 7/8	British Tourist Authority
p. 10/11	British Tourist Authority Sheridan Photo Library
p. 12/13	British Tourist Authority
p. 14/15	British Tourist Authority
p. 20/21	British Tourist Authority
p. 26/27	British Tourist Authority
p. 30/31	Chris Gilbert British Tourist Authority Sheridan Photo Library Italian Tourist Authority
p. 32/33	British Tourist Authority
p. 34/35	Sheridan Photo Library
p. 36/37	J. Allan Cash Ltd.
p. 38/39	Sheridan Photo Library
p. 40/41	British Tourist Authority
p. 42/43	G. Allan Curtis
p. 44/45	German National Tourist Office National Trust Photographic Library

Cover Photo's:
G. Allan Curtis
Brian Boyd
J. Allan Cash Ltd.

Frontispiece:
B.T.A.

Design/Production Susie Home
Text by John Monks
Illustrations by:
Isobel Lovering
Francis Swann
Nick Tebbitt